Photo by Georgia France

This book is dedicated to my lovely mum, Kathleen Green. With her magical sewing machine, she tirelessly supports my creative endeavours with her love and wonderful creations. X

This book is for anyone who has ever experienced an awful, jittery or nervous tummy before they went to school.

Special Thank you's

I would like to acknowledge all of the wonderful brains that have helped to bring my book to life. I am forever grateful for your fresh eyes, advice and for never getting tired of my Brainy Bunch chatter.

I am also remembering my early readers who took the time to share their feedback with such honesty and enthusiasm in the early stages. Of course, there are the hundreds of children across the North East of England whom I have had the pleasure to work with - their boundless energy has spurred me on my journey. I am truly thankful for the flurry of positive messages relayed to me from the children in our schools, encouraging me to publish my book.

Thanks to Go Well also, for sharing the Brainy Bunch journey with me. It has been an absolute pleasure.

Finally, I would like to thank my students from the Bounce Resilience Academy, who have taught me so much and contributed to the personalities of the characters within the pages, through the stories they shared. I am grateful for your trust and I am excited for you to be able to read your very own copy.

If you would like to know more about how you can improve the emotional and physical well-being within your school, then contact **Hannah@Hannahbellclarity.co.uk**

Hannah

About the Author

Hannah Bell is the creator and author of **The Brainy Bunch**. Through her work with children, teenagers and adults, Hannah realised that resilient children grow into resilient adults. she believes that the Brainy Bunch might just be the key to helping children develop their own resilience.

Hannah has a vivid imagination and has dreamed of writing and publishing a book since the age of six. She has learned to work with her highly creative brain since her imagination can often run away with her. Hannah has her very own **Brainy Bunch Toolkit**, which help her capture her ideas and keep her Brain Battery fully charged.

She lives with her husband Chris and three naughty dachshunds who keep her busy. Their daughter Alfreya is currently studying at Drama School.

Photo by Ian Weldon

About the Illustrator

Liz Million is the fun and bubbly illustrator of **The Brainy Bunch** book. She knows how important it is to get the right chemicals flowing if you want to be creative! She has been an illustrator and author for over 24 years, ever since she was a little girl. Artistic Liz knows the importance of continually practicing just like the Dendrites. She can often be found sitting quietly in her studio but also draws in front of large audiences and gets them all giggling and drawing along. Liz's brain loves to make other people's brains go wild with happy chemicals!

It is my pleasure to proudly present to you:
The Brainy Bunch!

Introducing our quirky family of chemicals and brain parts that help us to understand our brain and how it is linked to our body and our emotions.

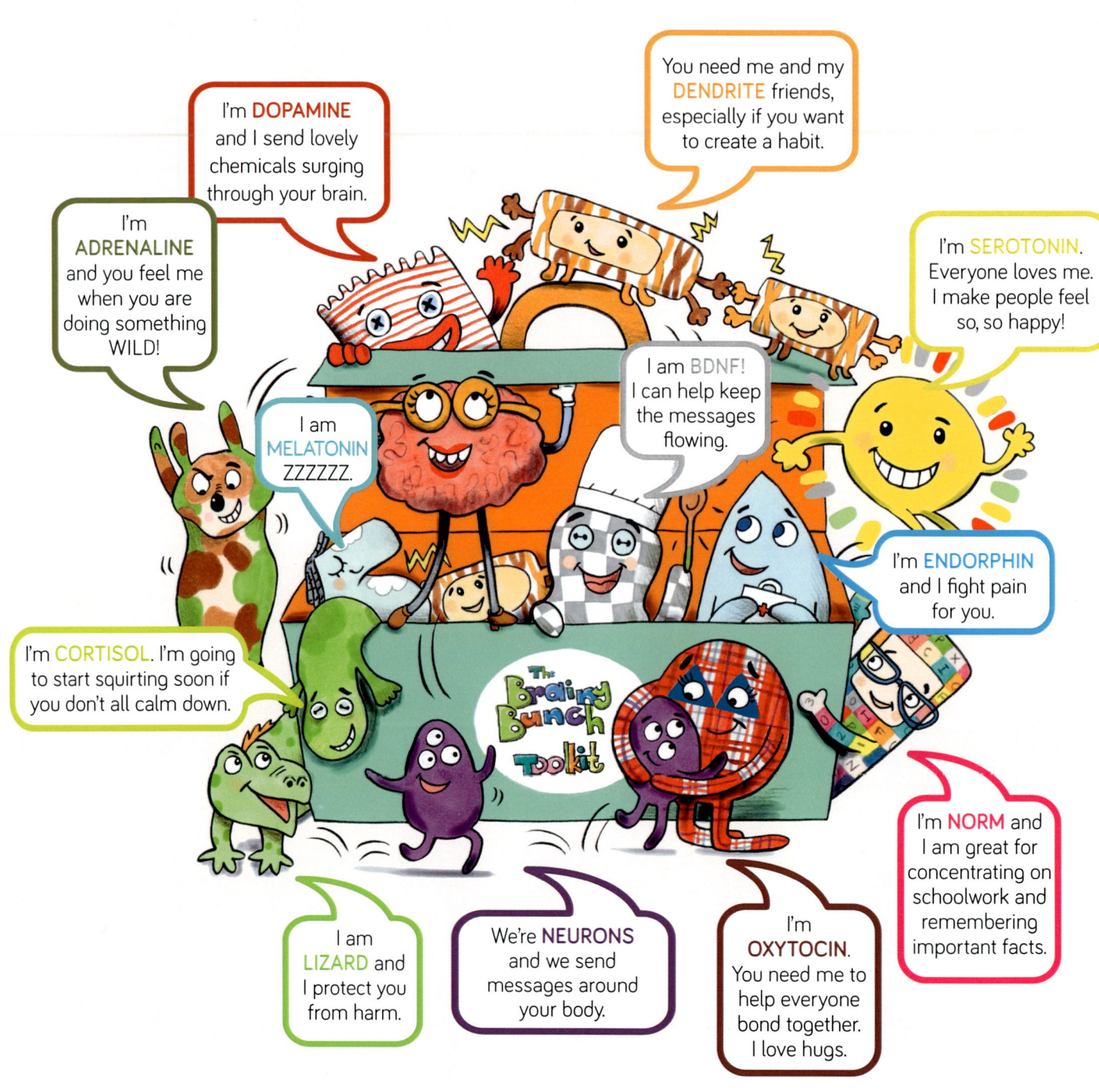

Welcome to the fascinating world of your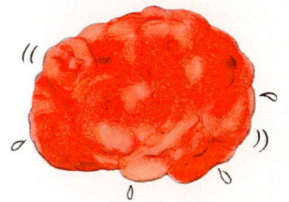

This book has the power to help you in so many different ways.

Let me introduce myself. I am Professor Brain, the smartest brain you will ever wish to meet! I'll be your guide; together as we explore your brain and meet some fascinating characters on the journey.

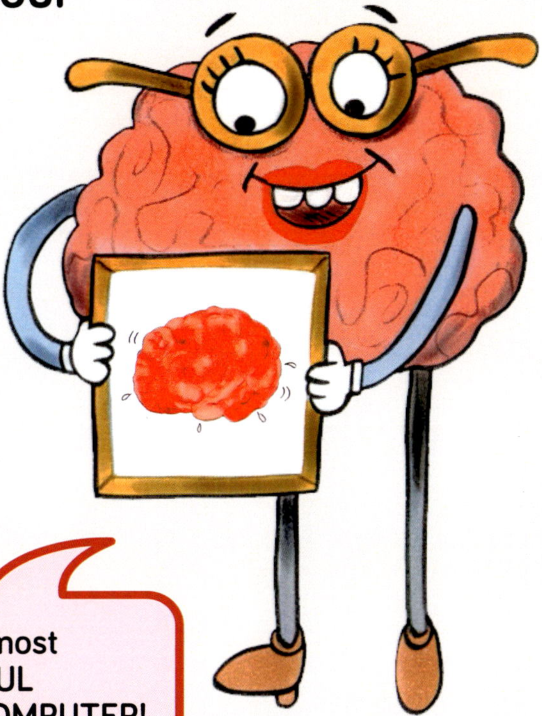

Did you know that your brain is an organ? Well, you do now. I'm seriously clever too. I may not look like much, but I am the most powerful supercomputer. Imagine the latest, quickest, smartest computer that you could think of; I can do even more than that and you should never underestimate me.

If you are reading this book because you are curious to know more about how you work, that's great! Or maybe you would like to feel calmer, or more comfortable around others.

Whatever your brain needs at this moment, you'll find it here. Each time you read this book, you will discover something new. We will have so much fun as we learn together!

I am the most POWERFUL SUPERCOMPUTER!

SIGHHHHH!!!

Shhhh! This book contains secrets that even some grown-ups don't know.

Every brain is unique, which is what makes each of us special and individual. Scientists used to think that our brains were hard-wired, or fixed for ever, and that we could not make any changes to it. However, even if someone has experienced unhelpful situations, we can still create changes. Brains are like clay or dough and can change shape and move with every thought. This is called **Neuroplasticity**.

Can we REALLY sculpt our own brains?

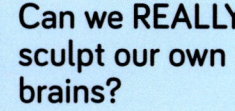

Being different is good, but sometimes it means that we don't always get it right. We assume that others think, feel, and hear the way that we do. But we don't! We all process information differently, according to our own brain. I am going to help you discover how to get the best from your brain and to help others to do the same.

- Have you ever felt sick before school?
- Have you ever felt annoyed or upset, or couldn't understand why a friend wouldn't speak to you?
- Have you ever felt sad or flat for no reason?
- Do you ever feel so cross that you think you are going to explode?
- Maybe you couldn't describe your feelings properly but just knew you didn't feel quite right.

You are your very own Mood Meter. How do you feel right now, in this moment?

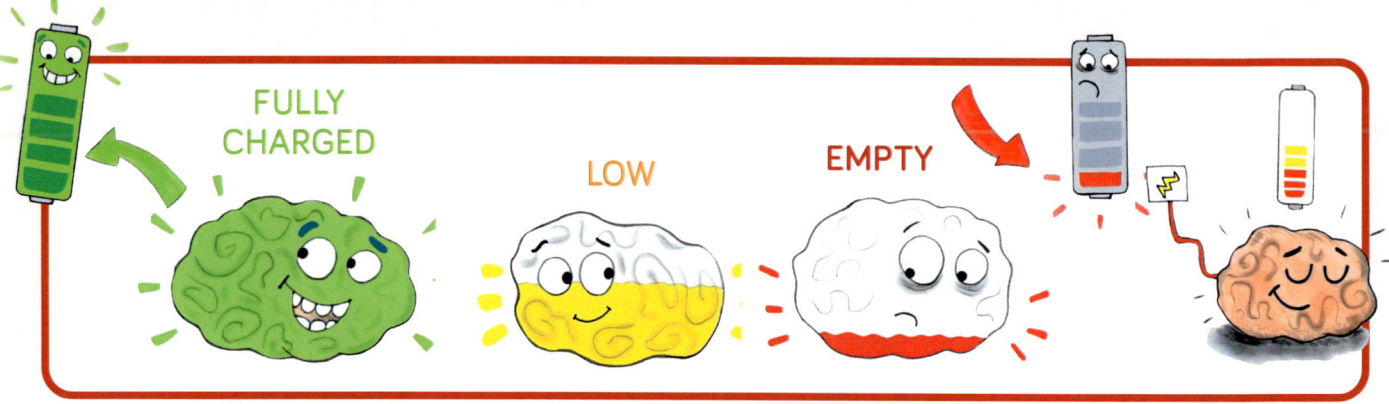

If you feel happy, that's great! Enjoy it! Maybe think about what you have just experienced to feel like this. Were you kind to someone who looked sad? Have you just eaten some healthy fruit? Did you know that both those activities charge up your Brain Battery? When your Brain Battery is charged, you will start to feel the effects on your Mood Meter. Did you know you can charge your own Brain Battery?

If you check in with the Mood Meter and you feel angry, then what can you do right now to change that? Remember that thoughts can become things, so take a nice big deep breath and count to five. Pause for a moment, and gently and calmly allow your breath out. Then count down from 5, 4, 3, 2, 1.

If we don't take care of ourselves and spend too much time playing computer games, staying up late, forgetting to drink water, being unhelpful to others, worrying or getting angry, we drain our battery. This can lead to our Mood Meters going in the wrong direction.

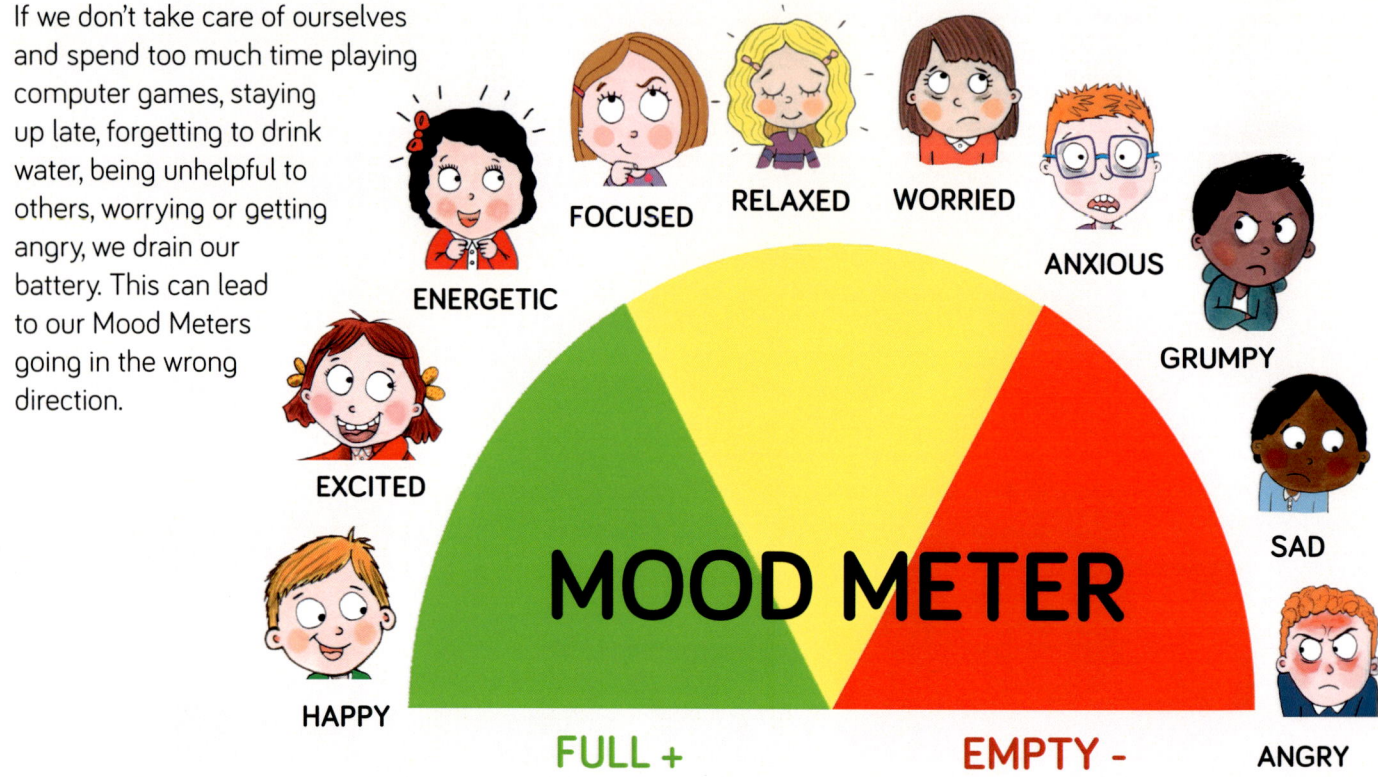

Would you like to know how to have more good days? Well, you have come to the right place, and isn't that helpful? I am going to show you how to work with me, your brain, to change how you are feeling. How does that sound? Are you looking forward to seeing who else is a part of this brain adventure?

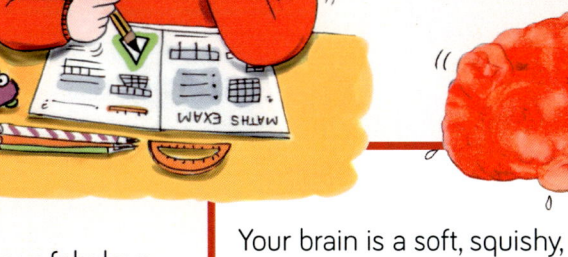

> Sometimes I feel sick in my tummy when I have a test at school.

The more you use me, your fabulous brain, the smarter I become. I am always working and on the go, even when you are fast asleep.

Your brain is a soft, squishy, wrinkly lump which sends signals to make your heart beat, your lungs draw breath and your eyes blink. Did you know that your brain is connected to every part of your body by a long network of nerves? It will weigh about 1.5kg when you are fully-grown.

Together, we'll explore your brain and meet some fascinating and quirky characters along the way. Are you ready for an exploration of the most amazing, wonderful, wrinkly organ - your brain?

> The tools and techniques we learn will grow with us as we get older.

> I want to be calmer!

> I want to be fit and run faster!

> I want to have good sleep!

> I want to like school and be smarter!

> It is my pleasure to show you the inside of your brain, starting with the first of the Brainy Bunch.

The more we discover, the easier it will become to work together with your brain and achieve amazing results.

Together, we are going to build your very own Brainy Bunch Toolkit. Inside you'll find everything you need, but you get to decide what is right for you.

Meet the team

Before we get up close and personal with the Brainy Bunch chemicals, I would like to help you understand what is going on inside me. Scientists are still figuring out what exactly makes me tick.

I am made up of many specialised areas, like a system, or a team really. Let's meet them now.

I am the Cerebellum; sometimes, I am called the Hindbrain. I live at the back of your brain in your brain stem. I am much smaller than the Cerebrum, which is also known as your Forebrain. While I may be small, I'm still very powerful so don't underestimate me! I control your balance, movements, and tell your muscles how to move together so that you can dance, run, jump, walk, play football and swim. I basically help you do everything, even your homework! I work very closely with my friend, the Brainstem, and we keep you alive by controlling your heart rate, breathing, and sleeping.

It is very important that we get along because we have to work together to keep our humans alive. We're very lucky to have good communication, as some of the Brainy Bunch chemicals do not always get it right.

Hello! I am the Spinal cord, a long wire that runs down your back from the top of your head to the bottom of your back. I receive information from everywhere, including all your organs, nerves, skin and muscles. I send messages to every part of your body so you can be the wonderful walking and talking human that you are. I know everything that is going on in your body and brain. If you touch your spine now, you will feel the bone that protects me like armour - that is how important I am. Did you know that some of my messages can travel 100 metres per second? That's faster than any human!

Did you spot how Hindbrain gave me a quick mention there? I am the **Forebrain or Cerebrum** to my friends and I'm in charge of your body's chemical factory. I organise everyone and coordinate how you deal with your emotions, such as reactions to being hungry or thirsty.

There are a few other brain parts that live with me, but, for once, I would like everyone to focus on just me. The chemicals and I are really good friends (when they're following instructions) but sometimes, I have to make them follow the rules as they can be quite mischievous. It can be exhausting when there are so many chemicals wanting to be in charge, all squirting and rushing to take over. Once you have read this book, it will be fantastic if you could help me to work with your brain so we can enjoy a calm, chilled-out life. Today, you are going to discover that you are the controller of your own brain. Let's get the Brainy Bunch working together!

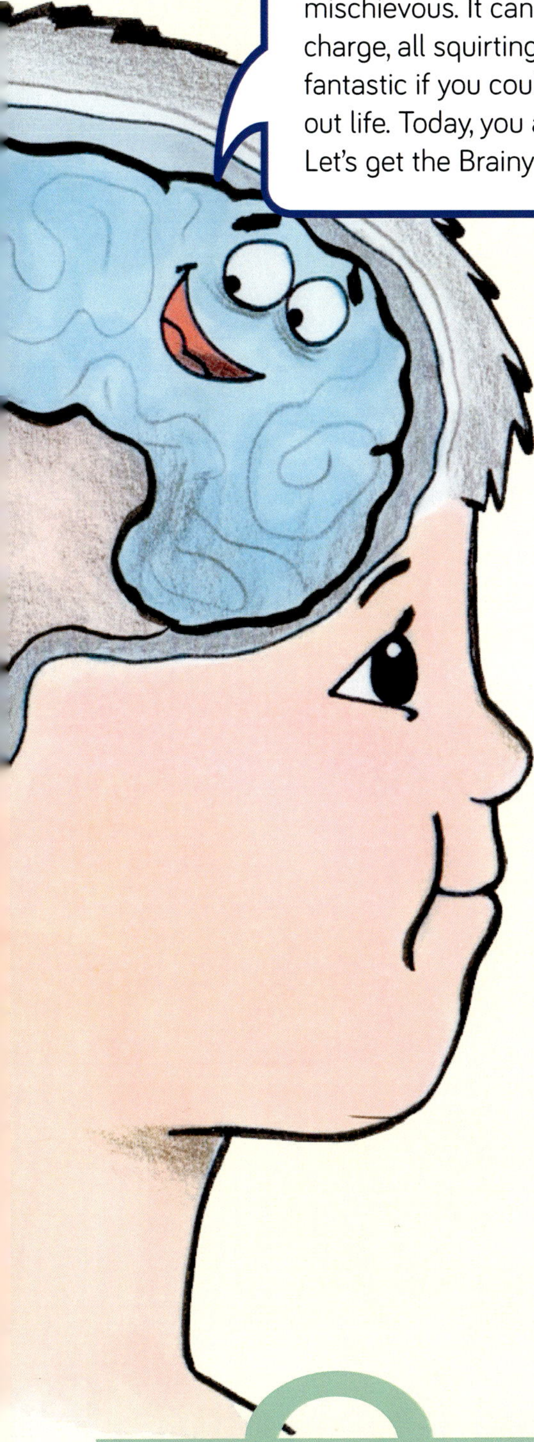

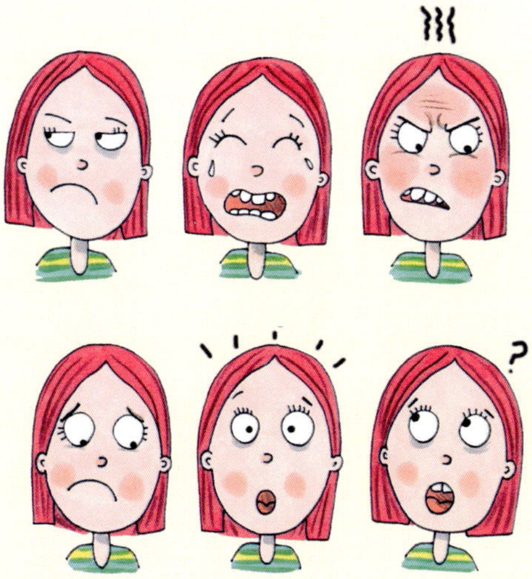

Would you like to feel in control of your emotions?

Check out The Brainy Bunch Toolkit (located at the bottom of most pages). It is packed with tools and techniques to help you work with your brain and charge up your Brain Battery.

Hey, I live here too, look out for me later in the book.

Meet the NEURONS

I have decided to introduce you to my friends, the Neurons, first. Why? Because there are so many of them and they can be so loud! Imagine your loudest friend who shouts when they are only a few steps away from you. Well, there are 85 billion of these booming voices, all inside your brain.

85,000,000,000 – Look at all those zeros! Did you know that there are 10 times more Neurons in your brain than people living on Earth? I do enjoy a good fact.

You guys are noisy today.

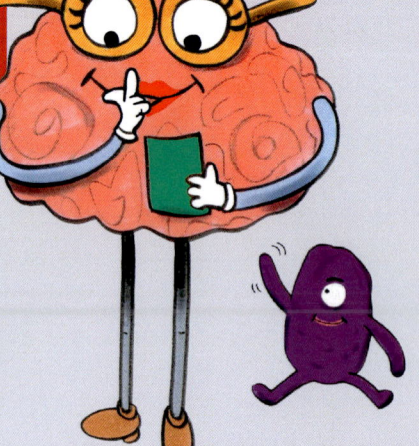

How can you hear yourself think?

Each Neuron is a nerve cell, and they will send messages around your body. You were born with lots of Neurons but very few connections between them, which is why you had to be taken care of at first. As you experienced the world, your Neurons created the connections and pathways that make up who you are today. Our brains are always changing and you can find out how to make the right changes to help yourself. Keep reading, we're already feeling the power surge!

There are exceptions; some Neurons know how to whisper, like when you are telling someone something that you don't want anyone to overhear. I have to say though, Neurons are very smart, and you need them to send signals to other parts of your brain and your body. They may be tiny, but they control everything you do.

We also learn when you make mistakes or don't always get it right. So, give yourself a break and then give it another go!

We grow when you do something difficult. We love a challenge because it makes us stronger – the trickier, the better! So, every time you do something different, it helps us Neurons to grow and become fitter. We love it when you move your body and enjoy physical activity.

We can send in the Brainy Bunch chemicals to make you feel different, which is why we want you to work with us to choose how you want to feel. We shout louder to let you know that the Brainys are on their way in. It's like when you use Wi-Fi with your computer. You can't see a wire, but the signals are still there. Some of the chemicals make us active, while others slow us down.

Neurons that fire together, wire together.

The DENDRITES

These are the Dendrites, our very talented and special friends! You could say that they are related to the Neurons, they do very similar jobs. They are like branches of a tree and help pass on messages to help you to create habits. Dendrites love repetition so they can work their muscles and become super strong.

> There are so many of them to please and they keep on growing. Every time I look over, there are even more!

> Move out of the way, this is my time! Hello! Hi! Yo! Right, here goes! Today, I am the strongest Dendrite of my bunch, and I am going to do all the talking.

We are best friends with the Neurons and we are the muscle behind them - the muscle memory. I know we look different from the muscles that you can see on your body. We are shaped like branches of a tree so messages can flow really fast. We help you remember how to do things so you can create habits. Today, I am going to help you to discover how to make these habits more helpful.

We are brilliant for making new habits. We know it can feel tricky or awkward when you are learning something new. Or maybe you feel clumsy if it is something physical. This is because a Dendrite is weak at first. Like you, it takes us time to improve. However, once you do become really good at something, like suddenly being able to ride your bike without wobbling, or spelling a complicated word, it means you've made your Dendrite really strong.

"Yes, and so bossy!"

"No wonder we get tired working with this bunch..."

"Mmmm, they can be so needy!"

"What can I do if I want to change something? I just love sweets, crisps, and biscuits. I dream about them and could eat them all day long."

You do have to work at it though. Have you ever noticed that if you haven't exercised in a while, it's not as easy when you start again? That's because we Dendrites become lazy and snooze.

You need to wake us up again – get us moving and energised. If you want to stop feeling a certain way, the best thing to do is to replace the old Dendrite with a new one. Take small steps towards your new goal.

We love your happy chemicals and, as you read this book, you will find out how to turn on your happy chemicals in new ways.

Once you have built a new habit, you'll be so pleased you'll want to create another. Practice really does make perfect.

Less gaming, more swimming

Do less of this ...

... and more of this

If you would like to spend less time on your computer games, then you need to excite us by creating some happy chemicals. Swimming is a great way to do this.

To stop feeling a certain way or to change an unhelpful habit, you have the power to replace old Dendrites with new helpful ones. Old sugar-loving and crisp-munching Dendrites will become weaker while fruit-eating, healthy, and sporty Dendrites grows stronger and more muscular.

13

The LIZARD

Allow me to introduce you to my friend, the Lizard, who is responsible for your survival and is constantly on the lookout for anything that could harm you. Sometimes our Lizards, also known as the Amygdala, can enter a state of high alert that can only be calmed down by other members of the Brainy Bunch. This is why it is so important that we work as a team to get the best out of our brains.

> You should have told them why I am called the Lizard! It's because I actually look like a lizard in your brain.

Let's remember, Professor Brain, that everything I do is done with good intentions, even if I don't always get it right. I can be overly cautious, sending in the wrong Brainy Bunch characters and creating unnecessary drama in your life. This might be when you feel a really strong emotion like anger, sadness, fear, or happiness. It can be difficult to figure out the most helpful response. Especially from where I am sitting (at the top of your spine near the back of your neck).

Working with me and discovering how to manage your emotions means that you can feel calmer, smarter, and have a choice in how you respond to things in life. When I am calm, together we can choose which of the Brainy Bunch squirts and surges. I fire off the signals to cause the different chemicals to be released. When I feel that I need to protect you, I act quickly, The Brainy Bunch jumps in, and then it's my show. Understanding this, and working with me, gives you the freedom to reach into your Toolkit and create the right chemicals to help you.

> Show us your moves Lizard!

> Well, I do have quite a few. Here goes!

FLIGHT.

When you find yourself in a situation like someone being unkind to you or not getting the right answer in class, you may want to run away from the problem. This is because I want to get you out of the situation quickly. It's a great response if there's a race but it's not helpful in every situation.

Imagining Dendrites growing stronger in your brain, helps us to become stronger.

FREEZE.

This can be a tricky one to explain, as it depends on how many of the Brainy Bunch are surging at the same time. For example, you may experience this zone when you can't get your words out if you are disagreeing with friends, or if you are asked to read out loud in class. The freeze response can be okay in small doses, like if you walk into your bedroom and suddenly can't remember why you are there. I bet the adults you live with do this all the time. It can also be very annoying when I have frozen you and you would rather be doing something else.

FIGHT.

When you are in real danger, you need this Lizard move. I send in Adrenaline and Cortisol to give you super strength. Again, I can get confused sometimes and react badly so you might suddenly feel like you have a lot of anger for no reason. However, when we learn to work together, we can change my responses.

FLOP.

These are the days where you might have had lots going on and you feel heavy and tired. If you have enjoyed a super busy week at school, you should listen to your body and have a chilled out afternoon. It can help recharge your Brain Battery if you were to create a habit where you go outside for some fresh air and sunshine. This makes some lovely Serotonin to get you feeling happier and energised.

FRIEND.

This is my favourite lizard move because here we are working in harmony and getting the best from each other. You are in the driving seat and I am calm, listening to you about how you would like to feel, think and behave. Always know that my beady lizard eyes are on the lookout for anything that requires me to take action and look after you though. So enjoy this wonderful feeling, knowing that I am there for you. What a perfect balance it is, for a human and a Lizard to enjoy their life together, being respectful and understanding of each other.

If you recognise that I have taken over in an unhelpful way, you have a choice in how you'll react. Breathing techniques are a great way to get calm and remind yourself that you are in control. Think about the best possible outcome. Even a pause can help. Other helpful activities include listening to calming music or breathing in lovely smells close by. Lizards also love routines, so a calendar or noticeboard keeps me in the 'friend' zone. A great thing about helpful habits is that it means you are building helpful Dendrites. Imagining or visualising them growing stronger and working together can create positive habits.

The Happy Chemical Bunch

The happy chemical bunch have been bouncing around since I first welcomed you to our book. All of them are excited and wanting to appear first. I have made the executive decision to invite them in at the same time. They are all equally important and I just couldn't choose!

So, here goes: Welcome Serotonin, Dopamine, Oxytocin and Endorphin.

They are four wonderful chemicals who can boost your brain and how you feel. This is an opportunity to build new habits with the help of Neurons and Dendrites to make it easier to enjoy a calmer and happier life. There are other chemicals that we may meet later who help us to feel good and these are truly worth getting to know.
When they are all surging together, then there's a real party in your head.

SUPER WORK!

SEROTONIN, that's me. I am the brightest of the bunch and round-shaped to remind you of beautiful sunshine.

I am DOPAMINE. Hey, what about me! If I am running low, I can wake up your Lizard and put him on a state of high alert! I have a special shaped head to remind you that there are always ups and downs in life and I can't be 'a round' all of the time. He-he!

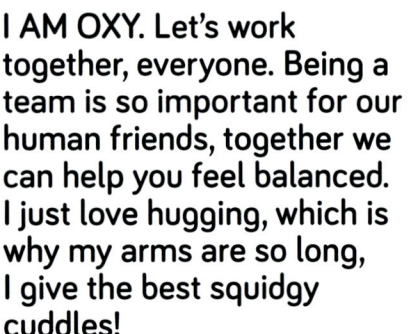

I AM OXY. Let's work together, everyone. Being a team is so important for our human friends, together we can help you feel balanced. I just love hugging, which is why my arms are so long, I give the best squidgy cuddles!

I am ENDORPHIN. I fight pain for you which is why I am shaped like a kite, so I can fly in to help you.

SEROTONIN
bouncing into the party!

I am here to make you happy. So if you would like to know how to change your brain chemistry to feel calmer and happier, then read on. Producing more of me supercharges your Brain Battery to green, which is just fantastic.

When I am around, I make you feel happy, especially during those moments where you feel proud of yourself. I love a compliment and praise. When you say something kind to someone, it allows lots of me to squirt in your head and in theirs too. It's a win-win situation! Feeling wanted and valued by your human bunch is important to me. This is why you often feel sad when you don't get invited to a friend's house for tea when others do. Playing games and sport outside helps to make more of me as well. When you are talking, playing, or working with friends, it is so easy for me to surge, especially when you are treating each other with kindness and respect.

I work closely with your stomach and help you to feel calmer, if you feel nervous before a test or when you are learning something new. Sometimes, if you feel a little strange in your tummy it could be a signal from me as I am in that part of your body too. Maybe your tummy feels unsettled, making you feel like you want to go to the toilet. Sometimes this feeling can even make you feel like you are empty and want to eat lots of unhealthy foods like sweets or crisps.

Recognising that you can change these feelings is so powerful. Starting the day off with a good healthy breakfast of fruit, cheese, or nuts, and eating it slowly gives me the best start ever. If my day starts well, then so does yours, because you can concentrate and remember important information at school. Then you can enjoy feeling super smart.

When you turn off your screens and stop gaming before bed, you will enjoy a much deeper and better sleep. I can get to work whilst you sleep and start producing as you dream. Then, I'm all set for my friend Dopamine to help you to jump out of bed full of energy when you wake up.

17

Meet the wonderful, DOPAMINE

"I know you are just going to love Dopamine. Watch out though! Especially if you have a sweet tooth, he finds it tricky to say 'no'."

When you are the first one in your house to wake up feeling full of energy, that's me. I give you a surge to get you out of bed.

Right! Here goes, the first squirt of me, Dopamine, is always the best. I am brilliant for changing your mood and helping you to feel calm, especially if you are in a grumpy mood. Exercise is the fastest way to change and improve how you are feeling. If you don't believe me, stand up and do five star jumps! Come on, charge up your Brain Battery. Can you feel the difference now?

I am the one who encourages you to eat another piece of chocolate, even when you feel a bit sick. I can be quite addictive which means you enjoy me being around and want more and more of me.

You know when you have that first piece of chocolate and want more, but the second mouthful does not taste as good? This is because my surge is less powerful. Enjoy what you have tasted and stop, because you will never enjoy it as much as the first bite.

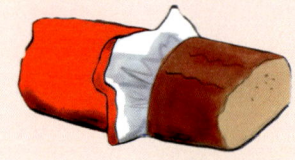

I squirt when you give a present to someone or receive a nice surprise. I direct your concentration and attention to help you get rewards and prizes, and I am always on the lookout for what makes you feel good. When I find something good, you can really feel me flowing. Thinking of happy memories is another great way for me to make an appearance. I help you to remember things as if they have just happened. It feels just wonderful, doesn't it?

Remember that being outside, even when it is freezing cold, is a must. I just love exercise, especially when you have a routine or repeated movement like swimming, dancing, gymnastics, or cheerleading. When you feel slightly out of breath, it's an opportunity for me to join the party. Speaking of parties, I also love music. So go ahead and put together a playlist of music that makes you feel happy and uplifted. Listen to it when you feel a little flat or sad and start a party in your head. This is great to do before school or during a Brain Break before a test.

It is easy and so simple to keep me around - repetition is extremely important because it helps me to wire the circuits so you can keep me balanced.

However, it is not possible to feel happy for every single minute of the day. Life brings us ups and downs and bouncing back when things do not go our way makes us stronger.

You will feel great when I am around, but watch out as it's me who can keep you playing video games for hours. I even keep you so busy, I bet you often forget to eat. I then drain your Brain Battery and you do not feel good. Everything in moderation is key.

When you have had too much screen time or have been stuck indoors all day, I find it really difficult to squirt. This is because I need lots of beauty sleep as it is tiring wiring circuits all day and screens stop me from working properly. I like to read a book before bed instead.

You need lots of me to concentrate and feel motivated to do something which you might not really want to do, like helping around the house or school work. It could be that you do not have enough of me because of too much screen time or not enough sleep. Check in with your Mood Meter; if you feel you are heading towards the red, you need to take action. What can you do to feel energetic and happy?

If you want to feel happier and achieve more, you have to change something. When you have an awareness of the changes inside your head and how much better you feel, you can build a good routine or habit. This helps you enjoy the moments when you are calm and happy.

Meet the cuddly OXYTOCIN

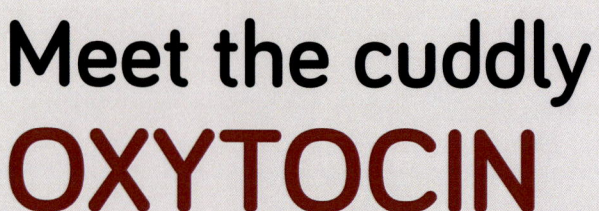

Here is my most huggable friend from the bunch.

I am feeling the love today! What a team we are! Hi, I am Oxytocin. I am all about creating bonds and finding people who like the same things. This is so important as I am a great believer that together we achieve so much more. I am connected to feelings of trust and I can help you move on from what has happened in the past to create a new future.

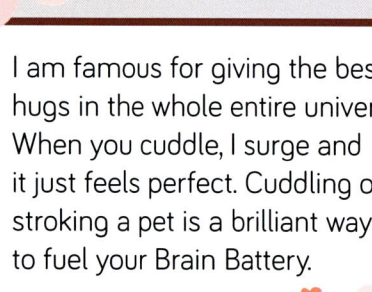

I am famous for giving the best hugs in the whole entire universe. When you cuddle, I surge and it just feels perfect. Cuddling or stroking a pet is a brilliant way to fuel your Brain Battery.

Did you know that when you cuddle a baby, it can make their brains grow? This is especially powerful when they are in a new situation or are feeling poorly.

I keep you safe in a different way to the other Brainy Bunch chemicals. Let me take you back to cave dweller days. Staying together as a tribe was so important. I made sure that our ancestors did not argue and storm off in a bad mood. They wouldn't have survived the dangers of being alone in the wilderness. Today, I help you to stick it out by encouraging you to return to school when someone annoys you or to not run away when someone upsets you at home. I love to spend time with family and friends and I help you not to judge people too quickly. It is important to build trust and get to know new people who may one day become new friends. I can be the reason you keep friendships with others and I help you to forgive.

When you have that feeling that someone really just 'gets you', that's me squirting and helping you to create bonds. This is why it feels good to spend time with the people who make us feel good about ourselves. Sometimes you can feel me when you are expecting a reward or about to win a game. I start to prepare to surge and if things might not always go your way, you will feel an Oxytocin disappointment droop. Check in with your Mood Meter and decide what you can do to turbo charge your Brain Battery to green. We can always change how you are feeling with the Brainys.

GULP!

I am part of the reason why people stay in groups that treat them badly but it does not mean that you have to just put up with it. Trust your instincts and if something does not feel quite right, then it usually isn't. Find a trusted adult to talk to if you feel like this. It is a brave person who accepts that they are perhaps not as safe as they thought. If you see someone else in an unhelpful friendship group, helping and supporting them is a really kind way to produce me.

Taking part in team games or exercise, listening to others talk or having someone read to you are all fantastic ways to create more of me. Another way is to share a laugh, smile, or even cry! Having a good cry is a way of releasing emotions so that your body returns to its natural state of calmness. So, let it out!

There are lots of different ways to create me to give you balanced emotions. You may feel a slight droop if someone breaks a promise or if friends let you down. But have no fear! Now, you have the tools to lift yourself up. My friends, Cortisol and Adrenaline, can start to become curious if your Brain Battery runs low, so keep being kind and keep Oxytocin topped up.

Fake laughing or forcing yourself to cry won't make me show up - I have to feel real emotion. However, you can start a pretend laugh to make someone else laugh and then you will often find yourself really laughing from your tummy. Go on, give it a go.

Fake it until you make it.

Get nutty, I love nuts!! Nuts are a fantastic way (if you are not allergic to them) to promote my happy chemical pals and me.

 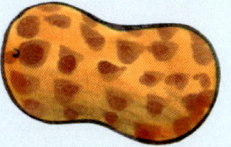

The more you move, even if it's just short bursts, the more I am around. We all need Vitamin D, as being outside in the sun helps to release Endorphins, so going outdoors for exercise is super helpful. It will also help increase your attention span and you will be able to concentrate and learn so much better.

You can't experience the happy chemicals all of the time. Each one of us will have a 'droop'. This is maybe where you have experienced lots of fun or surprises and then life returns to your regular routine. Your brain may be wondering where the excitement has gone and you may feel tired or sad. It is so helpful when you start to notice that we are on the move. It means you can appreciate us when we are around and then pay attention to the moments when you would like to change from an unhelpful mood to a helpful one. There can be situations in your life which can make you feel upset but how you deal with those moments will make you stronger and more resilient. The Brainy Bunch and the Toolkit are a brilliant way to discover how to become even stronger than before.

The quieter your mind is, the easier I find it to stay with you. Being mindful or meditating is great because it will help you to relax. This then lets you learn more, become smarter, and enjoy achieving in the areas you may have previously found difficult. Sitting quietly and being aware of your breathing is a fantastic way to feel calmer and to help me appear. It may feel a bit strange at first to sit and be still, but I promise, you will really feel the benefits. Soon, you will want to do it more often as it feels so good. It's like having your own magic pause button.

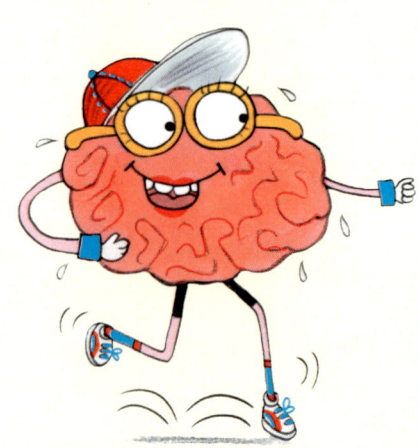

Hang on Adrenaline, wait for me to introduce you.

WOOHOO! I'm ADRENALINE

A good way to understand when I am around is to imagine how you feel when you are doing something WILD, like skydiving, or bungee jumping, or going on a rollercoaster at a theme park. Your body is frightened, so it anticipates pain because it doesn't know you are in a safety harness. When you see the ground rushing at you, your brain thinks you are in real danger and that pain is coming. So your brain squirts me out of your adrenal gland to come to the rescue because I'm the chemical that can help when no one else can. I feel really good. I like daredevils and people who enjoy rollercoasters. Do you? Have you felt me before?

You will feel me when you do something daring like riding your bike without stabilisers, climbing the highest climbing wall, or jumping off the highest vault at the gym. My arrival is like when someone steps on the accelerator of a car and picks up speed in record time.

Sometimes I get so excited, I accidentally wake up your Lizard to come out and play. The Lizard and I can pump you full of chemicals, and often your chemicals end up with nowhere to go. People tell me I can be annoying in small amounts because I help you hold onto unhelpful thoughts like mean words from other people, just in case you get the chance to retaliate.

Unless you know that I'm the one reminding you about the mean things others say, I can be tricky to shake off. I know this is not always helpful but it's what I do. So if you want to stop feeling like that, then read on – it's your choice!

I'll tell you that this moment you're in is important and I provide you with the energy you need to deal with it. I can often make you feel shaky afterwards, but taking control and returning to being calm will help you to feel like yourself again. I often invite my friend Cortisol to join in and then we never know when to leave you.

Sorry Prof!

24

Some people learn to like me, but generally, I am not a signal that something is good for you. It is the world outside tricking your brain into thinking that something terrible is going to happen to you, sending me in, to surge in to the rescue like a superhero. You feel my energy as I launch in to help you survive. I prepare you for action, but in most cases you don't really need it. Cortisol and I do like to visit but it is important you do not allow us to manage you. You have the tools to work with me, and I sometimes need a reminder of that because I can get far too excited, which could lead to you getting into trouble.

EEEEK!

WOOF!

Certain foods which you might crave, like fast-food, gives you a surge of me. You might enjoy them at the time, but I can rush out so fast that soon after eating, you may start to feel a little sad as I have gone away. I really love biscuits, cakes, and especially pastries. I'm not saying that you can't ever eat them again, but I am advising against having them every day. Save them as a treat and I guarantee you'll enjoy them even more.

There will be other ways of making a routine or ritual which will help keep you calm and focused. Remember, you have the Toolkit and discovering more about me will really help to teach me how to behave. In truth, you cannot and should not want to live this pumped up 100% of the time so it's important to keep focused on the fact that the feeling is only a temporary surge of a powerful chemical which should only last for seconds. The happy chemicals in your Brainy Bunch give me a place to go – which is out of your head! I can't quite believe how sensible I am being, actually giving you the tools to allow me to squirt in only a real emergency. I think the rest of the Brainy Bunch have started to influence me.

This is why we are in camouflage. It makes it easy for us to hide.

Well done, everyone, but remember we always have to stay alert for our humans.

We've finally got Adrenaline to listen to us!

When you practice and repeat something that makes you calm, I find it tricky to launch into action. Sending me signals to be calm through a ritual like reading or going to bed at the same time every night is a perfect way to keep me in check. Good habits and reminding yourself that you are calm and in control, make it impossible for me to compete with the other Brainy Bunch Happy Chemicals. They are a real force of nature when they come together.

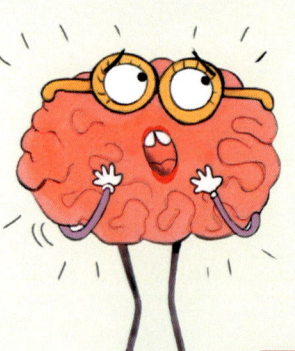

Hello, my name is
CORTISOL

> Why do I always hear you and feel you before I actually see you Cortisol, where are your manners?

I'm not always the most popular of the Brainy Bunch. I am your body's emergency broadcast system within your Toolkit. I am much slower to surge than Adrenaline and hang around much longer. You may find that Adrenaline gives you the first surge and then I move in.

Sometimes, if you are not listening to me or haven't noticed a message I've sent, I will get your attention by making you feel different. It's kind of an uncomfortable feeling I create in you which can vary depending on how much I squirt. I am so powerful that even thinking about a sad or unhelpful memory can trigger me. While your brain knows that the memory is not actually happening right now, I don't, so I give you a surge of the emotions you felt at the time.

I am a good friend of the Lizard and we both do our best to take care of you. Sometimes, I am described as fear or stress and often panic. All these feelings are because you have just experienced a surge of me. While it can be upsetting, it can also be a helpful feeling during a real emergency.

The Lizard and I aren't always clear on why we have been released. We can make you feel like you have lots of butterflies in your tummy, or your heart may beat faster, or sometimes you feel shocked.

I am not an unkind chemical - I am here to do what needs to be done to keep you safe. Learning to recognise me and working with me a little more can allow you to experience more of the happy chemicals.

When you understand my alarm system, you can more easily tell the difference more easily between the alarms on the inside (like when you're lost and I let you know to retrace your steps) and alarms on the outside (like when a car appears when you are about to cross the road and you have to stop).

EEEEEK!

These are really important as they keep you safe. I help you to recognise trouble before it happens, but sometimes the Lizard and I worry too much and we look for threats where there aren't any. This can mean that a tomato stalk on the kitchen floor makes us send an alarm thinking it's a hairy spider! I know this is not ideal, which is why understanding how I work is very useful and makes you feel so much calmer.

I am not all bad. I come in handy when you need an energy boost, which is great for sports, isn't it? I can also appear when you feel disappointed; maybe you didn't achieve the marks you expected in class. However, I'll then help you feel motivated to study smarter next time, so you hit your target. I can make you feel very competitive. Together, we get the job done right.

I can activate an alarm on the inside when you worry about something and sometimes my alarms are tricky to turn off. I am very clever and can spurt in your brain and your tummy from your adrenal glands, which is why you can feel strange in your stomach when you are worried or nervous. I am often described as a nervous tummy and, if I squirt too much, I can make you feel sick and sometimes snappy. I am always on the lookout for opportunities to protect you but I often get it wrong and make you anxious by mistake. Sorry! Working with me to create good habits is the key to feeling calmer and in control.

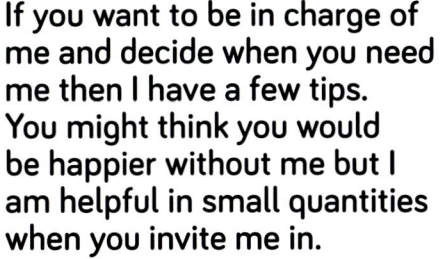

Are you ready to discover how to work with our friend Cortisol?

If you want to be in charge of me and decide when you need me then I have a few tips. You might think you would be happier without me but I am helpful in small quantities when you invite me in.

If you want to keep me away, I recommend eating less of the following things: chocolate, sugary soft drinks, tea and coffee. If you have fewer of these drinks and food types, it is harder for me to get inside your head. You don't have to stop them all together but just try to enjoy them as a treat. Bananas and pears are a fantastic way to keep me in check and they taste yummy, especially for breakfast.

Discovering how to manage me is a powerful tool for your brain. This way you feel calm, do your best, and keep well. It's easy once you know how. If you have been calm for a while and then invite me out to run a race, I can work at supersonic speeds. The calmer you feel on the inside the better. The more you listen and speak calmly, the harder it is for me to squirt. When you play calm music and relax, it is impossible for me to argue with the happy chemicals from the Brainy Bunch. When you drink lots of water and go to bed without technology, there is no way I can make an appearance. Enjoy your lovely sleep, I know when I am not wanted.

NORM - Norepinephrine

Here he is always on time and patiently waiting for his turn.

Oh hello, I'm NOREPINEPHRINE. I am usually one of the last chemicals to get a mention, probably because no one wants to pronounce my real name. So you can call me Norm for short, unless you are feeling super smart like me and want to know how to say it. Let's separate it and sound it out together No-rep-inefrin. That is just brilliant, you are a genius!

I am known as the chemical who is okay in small doses. I am a neurotransmitter, which means I send signals between nerve cells. I do sometimes get a little overanxious and wake up your lizard but this is because I am part of your flight and fight response that has been around since the prehistoric times. You don't want too much of me as I can make you feel all twitchy and fidgety; you might feel unable to sit still and listen.

I get your brain mobilized and ready for action, sending signals to your body at warp speed. As long as you know about me you can keep me in check. I am a real motivator, in a quiet dignified way unlike some of my other friends.

Do you ever feel worried about something and feel sad or low, maybe where you feel a little problem has suddenly become a big one and you are not able to stop thinking about it (I often hear humans describe this feeling as flat)? Well, this is a sign that you do not have enough of me. If you want to feel better then you need to take action! It's so important to get the balance right with me. I am great for motivating you to try new things and to stretch your comfort zone. I am great for concentration and I can keep you on track and focused while studying. I am very organised and a great time keeper.

I think it's important when you are doing your homework that you only work for 15 minutes and then move, go outside, take a drink of water and then get back to it. I call these Brain Breaks, short bursts of anything you are doing, I wonder if your teacher knows this? I can keep you alert and on the lookout for opportunities to learn and grow as I am incredibly smart myself, but I am sure you can see that by looking at me.

Monkey business is another clue as to what to eat for a burst of me! Yes, you've guessed it. Bananas again! They're brilliant as they contain a special ingredient which helps to keep me at a level that is right for you.

Understanding you and what makes your brain tick is a great way to become the best and smartest version of you. Just you wait and see as your results and school marks get better and better. If I am running low my chilled-out friend Melatonin can't flow, which means you may struggle to sleep.

I release straight into your blood stream through your adrenal glands which are just underneath your rib cage; this means that you feel me quite quickly.

If you would like more of me then it's exercise that will give you the fastest change and biggest impact, to make you feel happier and full of energy. I also love protein, so any fish, meat or whole grains are a fantastic way to activate me. Chilling out and relaxing is a perfect way to create me. Remember I love rules! They are there for a reason.

28

BDNF Brain Derived Neurotropic Factor or Miracle Grow for short

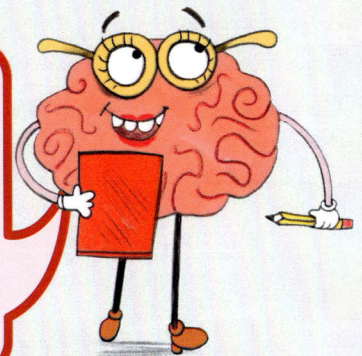

Our next guest is quite a diva and difficult to please. BDNF has many accents and is so flamboyant, but very important.

Bonjour, Hello, I am B-D-N-F. I am the finest chef in the whole of the human body. You will notice my exquisite chef outfit which I am so proud to wear. I create the finest culinary cuisine for the brain, mixing only the freshest chemicals. Some have called me food fertiliser for the brain. My cuisine is true art. I help all the important parts of your brain to grow. My delightful recipes even help you develop in maturity and intelligence as you get older. If you eat them, you will flourish even when you are really old and wrinkly.

I'll tell you now, I do not like that rascal, Cortisol. He rushes about through your mind with no care or respect! Yes, perhaps it feels good to have him around, when you are having fun but he can ruin my brain creations when I am repairing your marvellous neurons or helping them grow.

I am the Neurons' most favourite member of the Brainys as without me they would not thrive or survive.

You know I am not just a chef. I have many talents. I am a handy person/engineer, great for repairs and an all-round helpful chemical. Everyone here loves me, but you humans don't always recognise my true potential. I think it is because unlike some of the Brainy Bunch I am dignified and full of elegance.

It is not as easy to feel my effect on your brain. However, I assure you my contribution is essential to your brain health. You need me and the more you discover about me the more we can work together to help you fulfil your potential. One day even you can be as great as me.

There may have been times where you felt forgetful or a little sad and there was no reason for it; this is my message to you to make more of me. Sorry, but it's the only way I can send you a message, because you don't get a "wow" moment with me like the showbiz chemicals who love the glory and steal my limelight.

Have you ever forgotten something? Did you forget your times tables or a word which you have known how to spell forever? That's me sending you a message that you need to make more of me. You really should watch out for me more!

I am related closely to Norm Norepinephrine, not just because we both have names no one can pronounce or remember, but also because we are both growth chemicals. I am a valuable and vital substance in your brain, which helps your brain to grow new cells. I also look after the cells you already have, whilst providing you with enough chemical dishes to adapt, grow and develop new ones. My key areas are your thoughts, emotions and movement. It is quite a job I have but I can cope because…I am fabulous.

Like many of the chemicals I adore exercise, I am a little picky though and need you to choose a sport or activity which has repetition involved. For example, pick something where you have to learn a routine or play a particular role in a game. Netball, swimming or football are great. Dancing is a fantastic exercise and practising a routine is a brilliant way to keep me flowing. I shouldn't really tell you this, but I know that you can keep a secret. We are actually creating a Brainy Bunch dance and writing our very own song. Imagine having your own disco inside your home and brain. Aerobic exercise is amazing for you, so keep dancing.

MELATONIN

Hey there, oh excuse my yawning but I just love sleep. Good, deep sleep is how I make sure that you wake up refreshed, feeling smart, able to answer questions at school, make helpful decisions and most of all, being ready to learn new things.

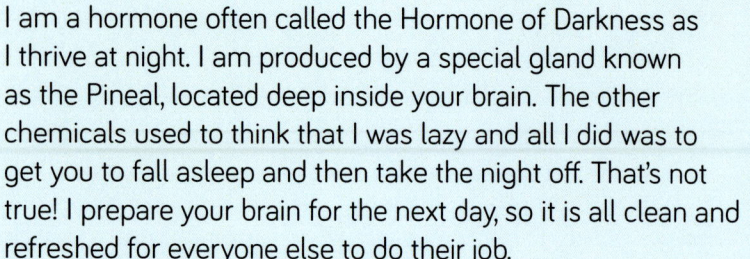

> I have left this sleeping beauty until the end of the book as they are one chilled-out Brainy. Welcome my friend Melatonin. Are you actually awake?

I am a hormone often called the Hormone of Darkness as I thrive at night. I am produced by a special gland known as the Pineal, located deep inside your brain. The other chemicals used to think that I was lazy and all I did was to get you to fall asleep and then take the night off. That's not true! I prepare your brain for the next day, so it is all clean and refreshed for everyone else to do their job.

My powers are pretty strong but there's a problem! Something drains all my strength. Can you guess who my archenemy is? I will give you a clue. It is everywhere, in your homes, classrooms, shops and even in your bedroom. You have guessed it! Technology! Mobile phones, TVs, tablets, computer games, Wi-Fi, they all create such a powerful chemical brain soup in your head that I can't get in there to help you.

> I am shaped like a "Z" as I love hearing your snoring noises when you sleep. When I'm working well, I'm surrounded by ZZZZs so I thought I should just be one.

It's Adrenaline and Cortisol who mostly stop me from doing my work, so we are not always friends. I only need your brain space for about eight hours. I am not asking for much, but those two little terrors would have you up playing on your devices all night long if they had their way. There is a job for all of the Brainy Bunch gang in your brain but understanding where you are likely to make unhelpful choices will make you self-aware. What a brilliant skill to have!

I bet my ZZZZs that some of you are feeling pretty smug thinking that you can fall asleep playing on your tablet or games? Well I have news for you! Falling asleep with technology is not helpful. It can really mess up the chemical balance in your head and the timings of your body. How can you be a genius at school if you have fallen asleep with exhaustion after hours on a computer game?

It is never too late to make changes you know! Try to read a book for an hour before you go to sleep or have a cuddle whilst someone reads you a story (no matter how old we are, we all love being read to). Believe me, you will feel so much better and brighter. Your eyes will be clearer and sparkly, your skin will be brighter and glowing, and you will be putting your hand up in class more often as your brain becomes a charged-up, chemical factory of knowledge.

Are you ready to get more ZZZZs in your life? Well, let's put your body clock right and get connected.
I need natural light, especially in winter, so go outside, wrapped up warm and I will be even stronger at bedtime.

If you have found that you are overreacting to things which wouldn't usually bother you then we need to make a start right now, as that's a sign your body is not in rhythm and you need more of me.

The fake light from your devices makes your brain thinks it's daytime; I can't compete with that, I am powerless. I have to wait and wait and wait until you put your device away.

This is something you can share with everyone in your house as grown-ups can be the worst for having their phones charging by their bed. Even lights from televisions or screens makes my work so much harder. So you can make changes together as a team.

Journaling every evening before bed is the best thing ever for me, I can float in, riding on my ZZZZ sleep cloud to do my work for your brain.

I love this idea, it means I can join in.

It takes only a few minutes to write down what you are grateful for and what has been positive about your day. This way you can enjoy a relaxing sleep and I am able to sprinkle my sleep dust. You will be training your brain by making a really strong Dendrite for your sleep routine.

It's a good idea not go to bed too late as even one late night can knock that body clock off. That's another thing you can teach your adults!

If you ever find it impossible to get to sleep at night and your head is noisy with Neuron chatter, push your tongue behind your front teeth and keep counting backwards from 10 to zero. This quietens the mind and relaxes your body so you are able to drift off to dream land.

Invent a bedtime ritual. Be calm for a few hours before bedtime.
Take a nice bath or shower. Remove all technology, especially smartphones and devices from your bedroom. Go to bed at the same time every night unless it is a special occasion.
Gather up your favourite toys, choose a book and get snuggly.
You could even try using super-relaxing smells like lavender to help you be as chilled-out as I am.
This is how to wake up with a fully charged Brain Battery.

Are you Toolkit ready?

> I need you to read this part very carefully as it is very important. You will have already decided who your favourite character is by now... or maybe I am feeling the Oxytocin flowing and it's actually me.

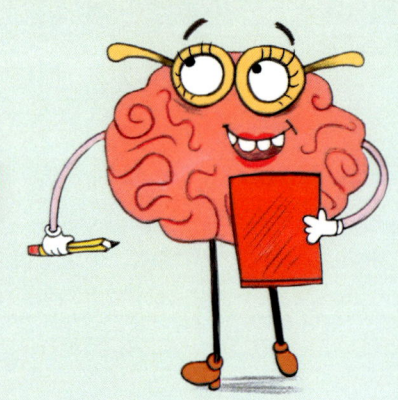

So now that you know how to create your very own Brainy Bunch Toolkit, how to check in with your Mood Meter, and how to charge up your Brain Battery. These are all powerful to use, and together, they are absolutely awesome. Physical activity and moving your body are brilliant for keeping your Brain Battery on green, fully charged and working at its best. You can discover so much about yourself by making a habit, using your Neurons and Dendrites to create powerful changes.

We are all individuals and that is what makes us so special, every one of us will have a unique Brainy Bunch Toolkit. You decide what charges up your Brain Battery and sends your Mood Meter in the right direction.

- I am curious to know which character you think you enjoy feeling the most?
- What is it about those feelings that you enjoy?
- This is what will charge up your Brain Battery.
- Which character do you think you need to create more of? How will you choose to do that? What do you need to do?
- This is your opportunity to discover what you need and what works for you, understand how to change them and make more of what you want. This could be learning how to relax or how to prepare your brain for schoolwork.

> Remember that when you do this with other people it feels extra special.

> Did you know that being kind and giving someone a compliment or even smiling at them can change your Mood Meter and theirs? How good is that Oxy?

> Why not think about a happy memory. Close your eyes and imagine being outside on a bright, sunny day, then feel really proud that you are choosing to feel calmer.

Shaking and dancing are another brilliant way to invite in some of your new Brainy Bunch friends to help get rid of your bad mood.

Did you know you have just super-charged your brain by reading this special book?

Stay out of the RED and in the GREEN.

> I just love a Superhero Power Pose: standing tall, feeling strong and imagining your feet are firmly fixed on the floor. Place your hands on your hips and make a triangle with your legs. Breathe in and feel those superpowers growing stronger. Look forward. SMILE. This is a great way to feel instantly confident. I often do this in a quiet corner or the toilet if I am at a Brain Conference.

> If you feel worried or shy, what could you do? It's not for me, of course. I am just asking for a friend.

Remember your brain likes to help you, so tell it what you want at the start of every day. This keeps all of the Brainy Bunch busy and working together to get it right for you. If you do not make it clear, your Brainy Bunch will not know what to do.

> Today is going to be a confident, calm day.

> Imagine you are asking a computer search engine to find something for you.
>
> Ask for what you want rather than what you don't want. Your brain searches for the most important word, so you have to be clear. You are setting intentions and your brain will do its best to help you.
>
> **I want to feel calm? ... I want to pass my test?**

> I am going to help others at school.

Here is your special formula. Remember that by playing outside, running, and enjoying fresh air, you are charging your Brain Battery. When you eat some healthy fruit, you charge it some more. If then you decide to read a book instead of playing on your computer, (yes, you have got it) you charge it even more. Your Brain Battery will be at super strength for when you need it. When you fly out of bed the next day, it's because you have turbo-charged your brain the day before. Look at what you can do to create that brilliant boost. Is there anything in there that I may have forgotten, that you do already?

Think about what changes you could make to keep your Brain Battery charged. Remember small changes have big power.

We would all love you to share your book and our tools with everyone you know. You and your family can share your Brainy Bunch journey; small changes, which supercharge your Brain Battery, can make a powerful difference to how you think and feel. Using Neurons and other brain parts, we can work together to make new Dendrites. Our friends the Dendrites, will then help the small changes become big. Tiny acts of kindness and recognising your strengths make a big

> Today is going to be a kind day.

difference. Imagine enjoying every day feeling happy, healthy, and calm while having lots of fun on the way.

What will you decide is right for your Brainy Bunch Toolkit? I think it will grow and develop with you as you create helpful habits to achieve amazing things.

I will say goodbye for now as I know that your smart brain will be back to read and reread this book. Each time you read it, you will discover new ways to have more good days.

Look out for the next book as I have some more friends. I would like you to meet. Thank you for being a fantastic curious explorer of your amazing brain.

The 'Why' of The Brainy Bunch

Photo by Ian Weldon

Hi! I am Hannah Bell and I am the creator of The Brainy Bunch. The idea came from my realisation that resilient children grow into resilient adults. I recognised through my work with children, teenagers and adults, that providing some real clarity about what happens in our brains might just be the key to supporting children to be in control of developing their own resilience.

My early career was in residential education. I then became a Police officer and eventually started my own business. Throughout this journey, I have always been passionate about supporting children and young adults to be happy and healthy. The Brainy Bunch feels like a real way forward.

My business, Hannah Bell Clarity, delivers workshops that help organisations understand how to use the brain effectively, manage well-being, and promote resilience through the blending of neuroscience, positive psychology, and neurolinguistic programming. Alongside this I established The Bounce Resilience Academy to support vulnerable young people who have experienced life challenges. This is a collaborative, multi-agency project largely funded by Social Services, Police Forces and The Police, Crime and Victims' Commissioner. The Brainy Bunch grew from all the pathways that I have taken and is now incorporated into the academy programme in a fantastic way, to help empower young people to make safe choices.

So many of the adults I meet during one-to-one sessions have spoken about how they experienced mental health issues as children, all wishing they had understood their brain better as they were growing up. My referrals for one-to-one private sessions with children as young as four are now at their highest levels. Our children and young people are in crisis. It saddens me that children are suffering with anxiety during what is supposed to be the most carefree time of their lives and all too often this carries over into adulthood. The Brainy Bunch is one way to tackle the problem, through early intervention and prevention.

The Brainy Bunch characters, personifications of our brain chemicals, help children and young people to understand that they have the power to work with their brains to change how they think, feel, and behave.

The physical characters were designed by me and brought to life by my mum at her dining room table. Personalities quickly developed to reflect the role of chemicals and brain parts, The Brainy Bunch is now in over forty schools around the North East of England and each school has an adorable set of Brainy Bunch characters made with love by mum.

And so, behind the scenes a book emerged as The Brainy Bunch came to life. This book will enable children to understand what is happening inside their minds at a time when they really need to enjoy calm, to lift a low mood, or manage anger and unpredictable behaviour: the possibilities with The Brainy Bunch are endless. I would like this to be one of those books that grows with children, starts as a picture book and develops into lifelong learning.

The Brainy Bunch programme is unique, its delivery compliments and enhances the social and emotional learning already part of the curriculum. I am hoping that the book will bring similar elements into the lives of more children. The programme accelerates EQ development, resilience, and self-awareness and provides a personal Toolkit for children and young people to manage their own mental well-being. I have hopefully replicated some of this in the book.

Go Well have been delivering The Brainy Bunch within education since 2017 and have supported hundreds of children with their emotional well-being. I am so grateful for their endless enthusiasm and passion whilst empowering children to create their very own resilience Toolkit. If you would like to know more about how you can improve the emotional and physical well-being within your school then contact:

Hannah@Hannahbellclarity.co.uk

What people have said about the book

The Brainy Bunch are fantastic characters that help children to understand their brain, emotions and behaviours. They are memorable, impactful and provide powerful knowledge and tools for lifelong wellbeing. We have witnessed first hand through our delivery in over thirty schools the positive impact they have on children. Now children can take the Brainy Bunch home with them and continue to enhance their learning and wellbeing.
Sarah Price - Strategic Director, Go Well

Understand yourself - have great relationships - make emotions work for you All of this and much more from a book that should be in every home, classroom or wherever there are children. This is neuroscience made easy - great tools and techniques to help people, young and old, be in charge of their lives.
Shay McConnon - Psychologist and Author

The Brainy Bunch have helped me to understand so much about myself and my emotions. I wish I'd known about my Toolkit and Brain Battery when I was younger.
Millie - age 11

A great way to introduce children and their adults to some pretty powerful information about how their brains work and how to influence chemicals and hormones to work for them. Every family and school need this lovely little book. I'll certainly be adding it to my therapy room library. All the best children's books have messages for adults too and this certainly does!
Brenda Oxlee - Teacher and Therapist

Serotonin makes me happy.
Ivy - age 4

Serotonin is my favourite, I know how to make more now to feel calmer.
Naimh - age 8

A very accessible and friendly book for parents and children to understand how our brain works and how through understanding feelings and the chemicals responsible we can choose change. Emotions are scary for children but I love how the friendly characters make it playful, positive and uplifting. Fantastic tool for working with families and looking forward to sharing with my colleagues.
Helen Kell - Senior Social Worker

Now I know why I cough sometimes and feel funny and what I can do to stop it.
Emmie - age 5

This has been and will continue to be a joy to read together as a family. My five-year-year old enjoyed a different character each bedtime and my 11-year-old devoured the book in one and keeps returning to it for tips for his own Toolkit. This is going to be our go to book for many years. I work with toddlers and it is never too early to start understanding our minds.
Lisa Braidley - mum to Jefferson and Livinia. Owner of Toddler Sense

I love this book, I like to read it and draw the Brainy Bunch. I have learned so much already. I like my brain.
Lily - age 8